I0140171

A Guide to the Soul

LOVE'S AWAKENINGS

Healing the Human Spirit — A Poetic Journey

By Robert Clancy

Mohawk Street Press
New York
FIRST EDITION

www.guidetothesoul.com

CATALOGING-IN-PUBLICATION DATA

Clancy, Robert Steven
Love's Awakenings: Healing the Human Spirit—A Poetic Journey
p.cm.

Summary: Love's Awakenings: Healing the Human Spirit—A Poetic Journey is a collection of inspirational poems, affirmations and thoughts to enlighten your soul.
[1. Self-Help – Inspirational 2. Poems 3. Spiritual 4. Motivational]

Copyright © 2018 by Robert S. Clancy
ISBN: 978-0-9859395-4-0

All rights reserved. Published in the United States by Mohawk Street Press. No part of this publication may be reproduced, stored in a retrieval system or transmitted in any form or by any means, electronic, mechanical, photocopying, recording or otherwise, without the written permission of the publisher.

For information about permission to reproduce selections from this book, write Permissions, Mohawk Street Press, 135 Mohawk Street, Cohoes, NY 12047 or email to permissions@guidetothesoul.com.

Cover, Layout & Design: Spiral Design Studio, LLC
www.spiraldesign.com

Spiral Design Studio and the Mohawk Street Press logo are trademarks of Spiral Design Studio, LLC.

www.guidetothesoul.com

TO ALL THE WONDERFUL SOULS IN OUR WORLD:

You should take comfort in knowing that there are beautiful people in every corner of the world, many who live in war-torn areas, who believe in love and compassion for humanity. You are all blessings and know that you are appreciated in unconditional love!

Dedicated in loving memory of

**Caitlin Clancy,
Cindy Wachenheim,**

&

Amanda Christiane Garbacz

Truly precious souls who graced our world with their love, kindness and beauty.

ACKNOWLEDGEMENTS

The path to the *Love's Awakenings* was not created by pen to paper or keys typed into a screen, but by the many kind souls, kindred spirits and angels I've met along my life's highway. I first wish to thank the universe for guiding me on my path to enlightenment. I thank my family for their unconditional love. I'm in deep gratitude for my precious soul sis, Lisa Winston and my spirit guide Dr. Joe Vitale for recogizing my light. Thank you both for your unconditional love and support. I thank Teresa de Grosbois and the amazing members of the Evolutionary Business Council for your guidance, love and support. Finally, I thank you for reading this book. Share your kindness and all the love in your heart with the world!

I hope you enjoy reading this book and that it inspires you to stay closer to your true life path and that it helps you recognize how truly precious your soul is.

YOUR TIME TO SHINE

I would love to hear from you about your life-changing volunteer experiences and your reactions to this book. If there was a particular quote that added meaning to your life, please let me know how it affected you.

Do you have a compelling story about a kindred spirit, a lesson in compassion, or a captivating view on volunteerism that has changed your life? If so, I invite you to submit your story to be considered for publication in future Guide to the Soul books.

Please send your submissions to:
email@guidetothesoul.com

For complete submission guidelines and online submissions, visit The Guide to the Soul website at: *www.guidetothesoul.com*

Share on Facebook at
facebook.com/guidetothesoul

"There's a beautiful sun about to rise in your heart. Let it shine!"

— Robert Clancy

HOW TO USE THIS BOOK

This book is intended to be a daily spiritual guide to enlightened thinking and the foundation for renewing your soul. The inspirational poems and affirmations in this book fall into nine categories: faith, hope, love, compassion, self-worth, peace, happiness, strength and renewal—all to help center your spirit in each of these areas.

Each morning simply read a random poem in this book. Then, before starting your day, sit quietly for a moment, meditate and reflect on the inspirational thought to absorb its deeper meaning. Think about how you will apply this ideal in your own life while you reflect upon it throughout the day.

Before going to sleep, take a moment to recall how you applied this affirmation to your life and to others. It is encouraged to keep a journal where you write your own spiritual thoughts and observations to bring deepen the meaning and understanding in your life. Enjoy the journey!

All poems, inspirational thoughts and affirmations in this book are authored by Robert Clancy. All photography by Robert Clancy.

THE OAK

Become the oak among all the trees;
Stand tall in the storms, sway in the breezes.

Forever growing, forever flowing;
Let the light caress your leaves.

Draw your strength from your roots;
Know grace when you grieve.

Feel the heavens above you;
Know they're always there;
Just believe.

THE FEATHER

I've become the wind, as light as a feather.
I sail on love's gratitude
where kindness is my splendor.

I'm so ever joyous my wings glisten the heavens.
I carry the scent of the flowers;
my soul forever strengthened.

Blue skies are my playground,
the clouds are my best friends.
May air be the grace
that helps your beautiful soul to mend.

I may arrive as a gentle whisper;
I may pass by to rustle the leaves.
I know you miss me terribly,
I've become the breeze.

THE RAINDROP

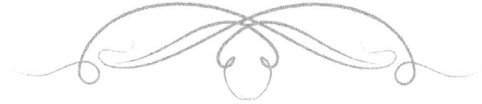

Become more than a droplet,
come join with the rain.
Fall into love's ocean;
release all your pain.

Swirl in this beautiful sea;
go with the ebbs and flows.
For this is where you're meant to be,
nourish the soul to grow.

You're born in the passing clouds;
gently fall to the Earth.
You quench love's undying thirst;
know your net worth.

Fill a chalice of compassion;
let it spill over onto others.
Be the dew on a rose petal;
rejoice for the lovers.

GRATITUDE!

Gratitude is a smile
wrapped in angel's wings;
It's the grace found
in life's simplest things.

Give thanks to the Earth,
impart praise for the sky,
There's no need to fret,
don't worry, don't cry.

Say a prayer for the hungry;
lend a hand to the poor;
Give thanks for your blessings,
fear nothing more.

Be empowered by love;
let it flow from your hands,
Know there's nothing more powerful
than the words **I AM!**

YOU CAN DO THIS!

Pack some smiles;
Gather love in your heart;
It's all you need to get your start.

Leave your doubt.
Lose your fear.
It's not just your day,
Make this your year!

Let go of the strife;
Make this your life!

THE STAR

A star gave its life so you could exist;
You were created from all its glory,
its dust and mist.

There's an entire universe of love that lives within;
Everything you'll ever need has already
been given.

Although this star gave its last breathe
for your soul;
Every ounce of light it's ever shined
is what makes you whole.

Some days you may feel like it's all on the line;
But that's just a reminder
that it's your day to shine.

THE LIGHT

Become the radiance among all the stars;
Shining your essence from light years afar.

You're the celestial rays all the angels admire.
Radiant, beautiful, your soul is love's fire.

Precious is the glimmer that lives within your eyes.
Brighter than the sun that embraces my skies.

Never cast shadows
for you gleam through the night.
You're simply adored in Heaven,
for you are the light.

GUARDIAN

I'm there to hold your hands
through the darkest of your nights;
I watch over your precious heart;
I'm the one who carries the light.

My wings are there to remind you
that I'm everywhere you need me to be;
There's no need to ever worry;
I'm your rock and your sacred tree.

My halo is the circle of love
that's without beginning or end.
My love is as infinite as the universe,
just ask and I'll help you mend.

I carry your silver linings,
you always have a second chance;
Lift your chin up to the heavens;
let's start today's great dance.

LIFELINE

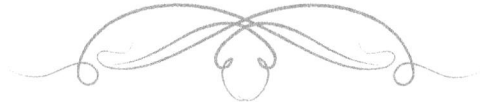

There is a lifeline in the Universe
that connects us all together;
Some think it's too heavy to carry,
but it's as light as a feather.

A shimmering miracle
they call God's golden strand;
Its reach is infinite,
its power truly grand.

When life has left you battered and bruised,
It just takes one prayer;
for it's something you choose.

Even if you're all the way at the end of your rope;
This precious lifeline is the grace we call hope.

THE TREE

A tree respects its roots so it can grow tall above the canopy.
It knows it needs to reach for the light,
beyond what it cannot see.

Branches grow to touch others
while its beautiful leaves flow in the breeze.

It sways in the passing storms
as it shelters the weaker at its knees.

With every passing season just keep growing
so you'll be as strong as one of those trees.

A BEAUTIFUL SOUL

You're over thirteen billion years in the making;
You're special, I know this to be true.
Your soul dances among the moonbeams;
Your breath inspires the morning dew.

You were born with love created from stardust;
Your light will forever shine in the heavens.
Your journey through life's trials and tribulations,
will be your only lessons.

Don't take your travels lightly,
for you need to make your mark.
Step out of the shadows toward the light;
never look back at the dark.

Share all of your heart as you go;
Leave everyone with a beautiful smile.
For this is the road to Heaven;
Enjoy every one of those miles.

WAVES OF LOVE

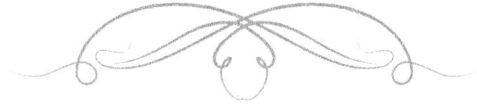

The sea of love is endless,
it touches everyone's shore;
You only need to open your heart
to let your kindness pour.

It's made from ripples of compassion
that flow with radiant smiles;
You may swim in it for a few minutes,
but it's better to sail on it for miles.

Although it may ebb and flow,
the waves will never stop coming;
Set you heart sailing today
for you should never stop loving.

THE ROSE

A beautiful rose has been placed upon my soul;
Light dances on its petals;
it's what makes me whole.

Its scent is infectious as a smile from a child;
Divine love in the wind is what makes it grow wild.

It becomes more resilient
with every passing storm;
Its beauty alone rises above the sea of thorns.

The light it brings to the world
helps everything renew;
For that beautiful flower
is love I found within you.

MOTHERS

There's a beautiful rose you're given in this life;
She takes away your hurts;
she comforts your strife.

On your birthday she gave you
the first smile you'd ever seen;
For any love locked in her heart;
you've always had the key.

There's more beauty in her soul,
it's like that of no other;
For this precious flower
is the one we call our mother.

ANGELS AMONG US

There are angels among us;
we encounter them everyday.
They may not have wings,
but they'll surely light our way.

Smiles are what they handout;
kindness is all they'll ever give.
They're the ones who make life better;
they're the one's who help us live.

Kind words always flow from their lips;
love continuously pours from their hearts.
They're the ones who are always by our side,
especially during our new starts.

We don't have to look hard to find them;
we already know who they are.
They're the people we call our heroes;
they're heaven's bright shining stars.

RAIN

The Earth was always disappointed because it could never touch the sky. All it could do was watch while the beautiful clouds rolled by.

Then the sky became upset for it could never join with the ground. It was never content with its beautiful blue color, so its heart began to pound.

The sky blackened with great sorrow and the Earth cowered in fear. For the sunlight they both enjoyed had all but disappeared.

The sky cracked with great thunder and the Earth shook from the sound; Flashes of angry lightening pierced the precious ground.

Consumed with overwhelming grief the clouds cried a great many tears. This storm raged on for days, but it felt like a great many years.

The Earth could not comfort the sky, it could only catch the droplets of sorrow. But when the light returned to the heavens, those tears had bloomed into flowers.

THE STORM

I felt I was forsaken;
my days as black as night;
Love was an empty vessel;
I knew only strife.

A storm had covered my heart;
I was clouded in life's blight.
My soul was in decay; I couldn't find the light.

I prayed to lift the clouds;
I prayed for God's repose.
A celestial voice called out to me;
I was given a heavenly rose.

Every storm that wakes
will always come to a passing.
For it is only love's light
that is eternally everlasting.

YOU'RE A BEAUTIFUL SOUL

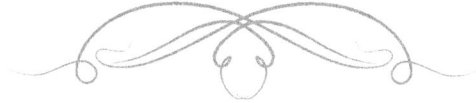

Your beauty is undeniable,
created from God's grace.
You're a true celestial champion
adored from a heavenly place.

Your soul created from stardust,
your heart is poetry in motion.
You're the light of every sunrise,
born in love's devotion.

Your soul gives love its voice;
your heart speaks that beautiful prose.
You're a masterwork of the Heaven,
created to help love grow.

Your faith will carry you through;
love provides the light of day.
Become that great beacon hope,
so others will find their way.

PATH OF LIGHT

Call upon forgiveness to release your precious soul;
Forgiving allows for living;
it makes the Universe whole.

Grace will light your way;
there's only one path that's true;
It's the one that leads to love,
the one with the heavenly views.

You may have shared your heart;
you may have some regrets;
But the greatest plan for your soul hasn't even happened yet.

Stay true to who you are;
don't give up on life's fight.
It will all be worth it in the end;
keep walking the path of light.

A PRAYER FOR YOU

May your precious soul
be comforted by a blanket of divine love.
I call upon the angels to watch over you
from the blessed heavens above.

May God hold you in safety,
so you can release your worries and fear.
Let whatever you're going through
be just a reminder of what you hold dear.

I AM LOVE

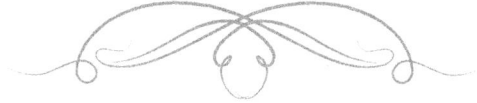

I'm the gentle breeze
that dances upon all the ocean swells.
I'm every single raindrop
that fills the living wells.

You think I'm far away in Heaven,
but that place is in your heart.
I'm always right there beside you;
nothing can keep us apart.

There's no need to live in fear;
there's nothing to ever fret.
It's time to live outside the shadows;
time to live without regret.

Every night I wrap around you;
I'm there to catch your tears.
I've become love to comfort you
for all your remaining years.

34

HEAVEN

Rest assured there is a Heaven,
just as sure as the Earth.
Love beyond your dreams;
love for all your worth.

The angel's songs are endless,
smiles are all you'll ever see.
Today you can let go of fear;
today you can let it be.

There's no need to ever worry;
you've already been forgiven,
Today, yes today,
is the day to simply start living.

BECOME LOVE

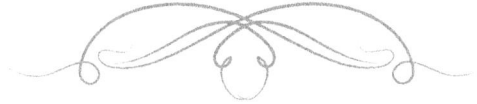

Radiate beauty;
become the petals of a delicate flower;
Beyond the illusions of time,
beyond all the hours.

Bend toward the light;
sway with the winds of change;
Reach with your heart;
love is always in range.

The sweet scents of compassion
will always fill the air;
Wrap your hands around someone
to let them know you care.

Stop looking...for it is how you will finally see.
Stop listening...for it is how you will finally hear.

Let your heart bend in the winds of change.
Be still in your beautiful soul
for it is how you will know peace.

WORTHY

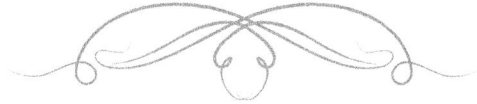

You're worthy of that second chance;
Just pray for grace to start that dance.

We all carry some terrible mistakes;
Forgiving yourself is what it takes.

Release the sorrows of your shadowy past;
Divine love surrounds you—it's infinitely vast.

You can heal your battered soul;
Just open your heart to be made whole.

TEMPEST

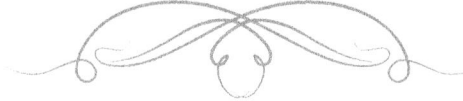

Your heart may pound with the thunder;
Your tears may fall with the rain;
You may shake your fists at the lightening;
Questioning why you were dealt this pain.

Storms of heart may come upon you;
Tempests befall you without reason;
No matter what happens there's a plan;
It's more beautiful than any season;

Trust that you're always loved;
Believe in that heavenly place;
Trust the storms will all pass;
For that is God's plan of grace.

LOVE NEVER DIES

The day Heaven called you,
I dropped to my knees.
I cursed the blessed daylight.
I screamed at the swaying trees.

The sunrise brought me no comfort.
Clear skies just made me blue.
I just needed a little more time.
There was so much more I needed to say to you.

I longed for your beautiful smile,
And that sparkle in your eyes.
My heart had fallen silent,
Only clouds filled my skies.

I prayed for my soul's solace.
I prayed for all God's love and grace.
The angels sent me a message;
You were taken to that beautiful place.

RENEWAL

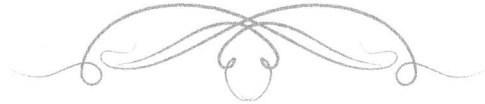

You're a one-of-a-kind original
created from stardust and light.
Let nothing hold you back;
call upon the angels to help you take flight.

Raise your hands to Heaven;
give thanks for the preciousness that's you.
What's past is just that;
the time is now for your great renewal.

All the love you've ever shared
has multiplied beyond your greatest dreams.
Any darkness that surrounds you is just an illusion;
it's never what it seems.

Rejoice for God's splendor;
your soul has always known its place.
Rise above; raise your spirit,
for it's you who carries His grace.

BE RENEWED

A radiant smile to light this new day;
Lift your spirit; you'll find your way.

Today's gift is your glorious second chance;
Start renewed; you'll find your dance.

Grace-filled hope holds each of your hands,
Divine love has more for you; it's all been planned.

Know you're loved deeply; release all despair;
At the very least, know I'll always care.

TRUE ORIGINAL

You're a true original,
Not meant to live in sorrow;
Raise your chin up to the stars
For there will be a beautiful tomorrow.

Be authentic and pure,
For it's where love breaks its dawn;
Cascade your light over others;
This is why you were born.

All the mysteries within your soul;
Everything that's been untold;
Genuine love to be discovered;
Let heavenly light be what you unfold.

TREASURE

Glorious is your soul, filled with riches untold;
But none of this wealth can be bought or sold.

The diamonds you hold are all within your heart;
Precious are your gifts; divinely created art.

All this beauty resides behind your beautiful eyes.
Endless love to fill the heavenly skies.

Your treasure is one that's meant to be shared;
Give it freely with complete loving care.

THE NATURE OF LOVE

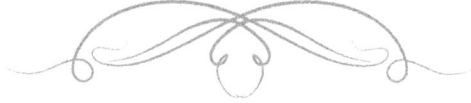

Listen to spring's babbling brook,
For it will whisper sweet nothings in your ears.

Turn toward every gentle summer's breeze.
Let love's solstice caress your face
with a warm starlit night.

When fall's wondrous colors surround you,
paint your heart in those shades of passion.

Catch every one of winter's
fleeting crystals from Heaven.
Allow the glimmering white beauty
to light your way on a cold winter's night.

Yes! Love is the nature of everything.

Rejoice for a thousand sunrises
have risen within your heart...love.

YOU'RE HELD

I'm empowered; I am light.
Give me hope through the darkest night.

Make me strong; keep me safe.
Hold my heart in the deepest faith.

Divine love; carry me in your hands.
Show me my soul is part of something grand.

Let me see I'm special; caress my face;
Showered in love with all God's grace.

ANGELS

Say but one prayer for the ones whom you care for.
The angels watch over;
you're the one they're there for.

Even in the deep dark shadows of despair,
Just breathe in the light they've abound in the air.

They know your sorrow;
they feel all your grief.
Hope is what they'll bring you,
so your heart has relief.

Love is all they carry;
rest assured you're never alone.
It's just one leap of faith to find your way home.

AWAKE

Start your day with a smile.
Open your heart to love.
Make a prayer to be faithful.
Know the heavens above you.
Love's great splendor, glorious grace;
Light of a new day upon your face.
Time for healing, time for peace;
Let love be your home,
Your heart has a place.

ABOUND WITH LOVE

There's no need to cry a thousand tears,
Never let the darkness rule your fears.

Today is the first day of the rest of your life;
No need to live on with any more strife.

Let love be your ocean, both far and wide;
Gracious God always by your side.

You're cherished, loved, adored and revered,
Abound with angels who are always near you.

Say a prayer; begin to kneel,
For this will call upon the angels to heal you.

BE GRACEFUL...
BE GRACE-FILLED

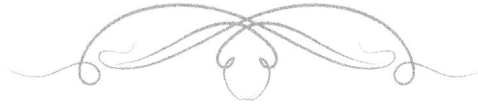

You haven't seen
until you've looked
through the eyes of compassion.
You haven't heard until you've listened
with your heart.
You haven't spoken until truth
has poured from your lips.
You haven't held until you've
wrapped your love around another.
You haven't lived
unless you've known love.

HAVE WONDERMENT

The vastness that exists
between every beat
of your precious heart.

The endless oceans flowing
behind your beautiful eyes.

The heavens reigning down
upon your delicate soul.

The grace bestowed
upon your wonderful life.

CARPE DIEM!

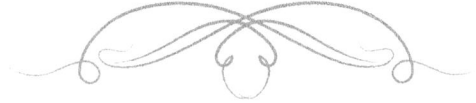

Rise up for today is a brand new day!
This one was made for you,
so the angels say.

Let go of your doubts; trample your worries.
Something great awaits you,
so you'd better hurry.

The dawn's light shines with grace;
the air fills with love.
Let peace fall upon you from the heavens above.

Take that step out of the shadows;
you need to be bold.
You're going glorious places;
it's been foretold.

Instead of just one day,
make this for the rest of your years.
Your precious heart is worth it;
go forth without fear.

IN THE LIGHT

Take me to the river;
never let me go.
Fill my heart with love,
only kindness to bestow.

Take me to the mountain;
release all my fears.
Fill my eyes with hope,
for the rest of my years.

Take me to the ocean;
let me swim in the vastness of your heart.
Fill my days without longing;
let nothing tear us apart.

Take me to Heaven;
let my ears ring with peace.
Fill my soul with divine light,
so all darkness will simply cease.

A MESSAGE FROM HEAVEN

I know you miss me terribly,
but this isn't goodbye or the end;
I've become all of love's beauty created in Heaven.

Everyday the angels sing to me;
I've saved you a special place;
Look for the hints I leave you daily,
for this is God's unending grace.

I know the love you've given me equals your pain and sorrow;
Know that I'm right there beside you,
giving you hope for your tomorrows.

When you speak to me I hear you,
even though you think I can't reply;
Listen for my loving whispers while your beautiful face caresses
the skies.

Know I will love you always.

LIFE'S BEAUTIFUL FLOWERS

Not a single one of these blossoms
will curse the dark of night;
For they always believe in dawn's dancing light.

Kindness is their aroma; sweetness is their scent;
Their souls are angelic, so heavenly sent.

Each of their petals, rich and beautifully colored;
They're often found together helping others.

Compassion blooms around them;
they wipe away the tears;
For these are the precious flowers
we call volunteers.

THANKSGIVING

Give thanks for family;
give thanks for friends;
Be thankful for everyday we've had
the warmth of the sun.

There are those we've lost to Heaven;
we miss seeing their faces.
Know we'll see them again
by the hand of God's great grace.

Be thankful we were created;
and that we've known kindness and love.
Everything to be thankful for
glimmers in the stars above.

Our hearts are infinite oceans
that at times may be on the mend.
Be thankful we all swim in that sea
to discover love has no end.

ANGELS WATCH OVER

The angels watch over your celestial soul,
From your moment of birth
until you grow tired and old.

Angels have been there
throughout all of your years.
Witnessing every smile;
they've caught all your tears.

Love is their gift, beautiful,
precious and rare.
But you're only worthy
when you've shown you care.

Kindness isn't fleeting;
it's more than life's goal.
A heart filled with compassion
is what makes you whole.

DIVINE MESENGERS

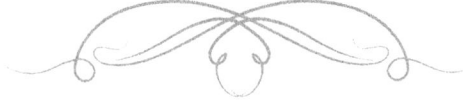

A precious light worker is with you;
one you may never see.
They witness every act of kindness;
only love can they foresee.

Divine messages they deliver;
each comes with a loving kiss.
They hold you through your sorrow
and rejoice when you're in bliss.

Their smiles create the daylight;
their hugs wrap you in love.
Every kind word you utter calls them from above.

You don't need halo to be one
or wings to travel so light.
Just love with all your heart
and say a prayer for someone tonight.

Let kindness wrap your beautiful soul;
From the day you're born until you're very old.

May you always know a loving smile,
like an angel's face;
Just whisper love's message
and you'll know God's grace.

ON EARTH & IN HEAVEN

Ease your mind, don't fret or worry.
God takes His time; there is no hurry.

There's a great plan for you;
it's always been in place;
The angels sing it,
while they caress your beautiful face.

All the love, everything you'll ever need,
On Earth and in Heaven has already been decreed.

Your soul made whole; you've been forgiven,
By the graceful love you've always been given.

SHADOWS

My soul was lost; what could I say?
No feet on the ground; no light of day.

Grief my dark pit of despair.
My heart emptied; does anyone care?

I know there's a plan; there just has to be.
An ocean of doubt washed over me.

My faith had wavered; hope was lost.
The price you pay when your soul is lost.

Mired in shadows; living in fright.
Is where I discovered God's beautiful light.

LOVE EVERY MOMENT

Open your heart; release your soul;
For this is what makes you beautifully whole.

When you're lost in sorrow or can't find your way;
Step into the light of this brand new day.

The angels watch over;
your heart they stand guard;
Life will become easier
after the times that it's hard.

Hold onto this moment; rejoice in your love;
For your soul is revered in the heavens above.

LOVE'S FIRST RESPONDERS

Volunteers serve others,
young and old;
They mend our communities;
they make them whole.

Their hearts are golden, shiny and bright;
They take to their work at the earliest light.

They don't think they're special
when they help those in need;
They just do what they do with love as their creed.

They're at every disaster, selflessly giving;
For this is life's best way of living.

LIGHT OF A NEW DAY

Smile if just for a moment;
let the angels dry your tears.

Time is just an essence;
let every second cast a year.

Today's storm will pass;
let tomorrow's light greet you with a kiss.

Bask in this loving warmth;
let your soul return to bliss.

RIGHT NOW

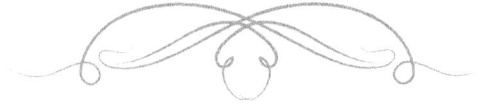

Release all your fears on the wings of a dove;
Raise up your chin to the heavens above.

Yesterday's worries to be left in the past;
Know that love will eternally last;

Tomorrow's doubts are never allowed,
When you live for today, empowered with now.

OCEANS

Let the kindness in your eyes
be as deep as the ocean is blue;
Allow the world to see the beauty
that's inside of you.

Let your heart be the place of only love's splendor;
Call upon the angels to be its greatest defender.

Let your soul be as peaceful
as the mountains are grand;
Be still in your heart
to embody love's helping hand.

HEALING

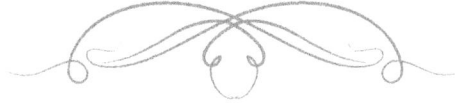

When you can't let it be;
Love will set you free.

When you don't know how to feel;
Hope will always heal.

When you don't know what to say;
Drop to your knees and pray.

LET LOVE...

Let love fill your eyes with wonderment when you see only the beauty that surrounds you.

Let love fill your ears with appreciation when you hear only the sounds of life's wonderful music.

Let love fill your voice with gratitude when you speak only words of kindness.

Let love fill your arms with gratefulness when they're wrapped around another.

Let love become you.

SORROW

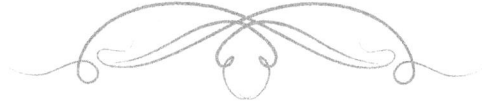

My heart so heavy with grief, I cannot deny;
I can barely see the mountain on high.

You're in the valley on a path toward the light;
I wish your fragile body
could give us one more fight.

I know I'll see you once again;
But that will only be in the hallways of heaven.

Maybe God needs an angel or another star;
No better choice could have been made by far.

I wish you didn't have to leave so soon;
With faith, love and hope, I will try to carry on.

God holds your hand with the angels in Heaven,
My love is forever I can only go on livin'.

SWEET GRACE

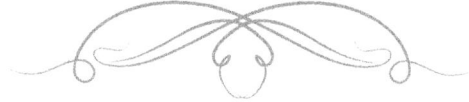

Nothing is sweeter;
Amazing Grace;
The sound of your heart;
A place of peace.

I could be lost;
Love has found;
A heavenly place;
I'm homeward bound.

Grace is the word;
I do believe;
Angelic voice;
It's all I heard.

Freed from fear;
Grace saved my soul;
A life rejoiced;
I'm finally whole.

GRACEFUL LOVE

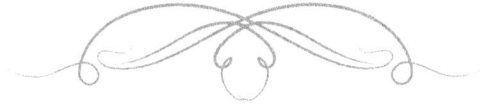

Grace is a gentle whisper in the wind;
Be still in your heart to let love in.

Grace will save you in times of trouble;
Just one prayer and your love will double.

Grace is with you for all time;
Love unconditionally; leave hated behind.

Grace is simply part of God's will;
Love is always there for life to fulfill.

THE BREAD OF LIFE

Blood is thicker than water
Bread is nourishment for life
Love will forever sustain you
While you toil through strife.

Don't give up or cower
Kindness is in the air
The angels watch over you always
With pride and loving care.

God knows all His children
Your name is etched on His palm.
Be still in your heart to know Him
For peace is your soul's calm.

STRENGTH

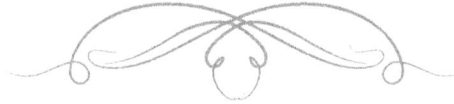

Give me strength, shower me in peace.
Free me from doubt, let my fears release.

A second chance, a wanton need.
An angel's blessing, what God decrees.

The light of faith, a heavenly guide.
I hold my belief, God will provide.

Life can be painful, forgiveness gets hard.
Divine love to heal, a salve for my scars.

God knows where you've been, held you with care.
Wherever you're going, God is already there.

TRUE FRIENDS

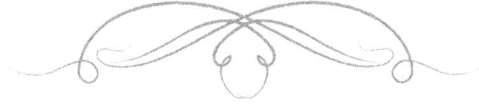

A true friend's love may bend,
but it doesn't break.

Their love always mends,
it never takes.

That's why I love my friends
for heaven's sake.

LOVE WILL FIND YOU

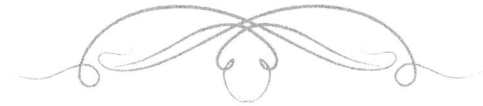

Love is a warm ray of light
beaming from the sun;
It may be found in the laughs
you've created by simply having fun.

Love may be written
within the kindness of your face;
It's surely in everything created
with all of God's grace.

Love is an endless ocean flowing
from each of our souls;
It's the greatest part of life
that completes and makes you whole.

Love can save you from
your deepest depths of despair;
It can never be taken, only given and shared.

Love is forever growing
within a community that cares.
It can start in modest ways,
often with just one basic prayer.

Love is much more than a smile
or just a simple kiss;
It's the legacy of kindness
given that creates God-given bliss.

LOVE'S SECOND CHANCE

You may wonder how far the east is from the west;
You may try to separate the worst in you from the best;
What's truly in your heart makes you unique from the rest.

You may struggle to know what to think or say;
You may wish for a brighter better day;
The answers will always come when you pray.

You may scream at the hand you've been given;
You may think no one knows you in heaven;
Everything you've done, God has already forgiven.

Life is more than a journey into the great expanse;
Hope is more than learning a new dance;
Just love, for God has given you a second chance.

LOVED ONES LOST

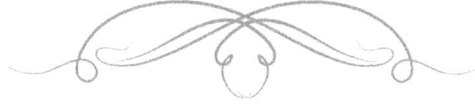

Without you life has been arduous;
I miss your smiling face;
There's now a hole in my heart;
a dark and empty space.

The holidays are hardest,
especially at the end of the year;
Hardly a day goes by where I haven't shed a tear.

Sometimes I regret all of the things
I never got to say;
Each morning I pull myself together
to face another day.

I take comfort in knowing the angels
now hold your delicate hand;
Although I wish I could change things;
it's all been part of God's plan.

If I said I didn't miss you, that would be a lie;
I can only smile knowing our love
will never ever die.

I know we'll see each other again,
but I'm still here in life's climb;
There's a place in heaven reserved
for us until the end of time.

PRAISE

I praise God for the light
and the sea of love
that surround me;
For even if I become blind,
I'll still be able to see.

I praise God for the roof
I have protecting me,
one that I've always known;
For even if I become homeless,
I'm still sheltered and left never alone.

I praise God for my family
and certainly all of my friends;
For even if I lose everything,
the love we create never ends.

GRACE

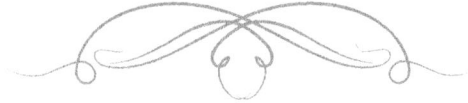

Be patient;
Be kind;
God is with you for all time.

Be not afraid;
You're never alone;
God will be there to bring you home.

Have no hatred;
Lose your doubt.
Love is what life is all about.

A whisper of peace;
An angel's face.
Share your love with all of God's grace.

WHAT IF...

What if the tender kiss of love abandons my heart?
Caring for others is a noble place to restart.

What if the seas of peace fail to wash my feet?
Divine love will be my retreat.

What if the rays of hope can't reach my face?
I'll just look for the light within my faith.

What if we all believed in God's grace?
Our world would be a better place.

THIS LIGHT

This is the light of a new day;
let it renew your soul.

This is the hand of a new friend;
let it heal you with love.

This is the rain of a new storm;
let it pass over you.

This is the darkness of new night;
let it fade by first light.

This is the way of God;
let it strengthen your faith.

SECOND CHANCES

My faith is as deep
as the oceans are grand;
My fate is inescapable;
but it's all part of God's plan.

Life could be simple,
But often it's hard.
Hope is God's grace;
Leading my charge.

I pray for peace;
I pray for a lot.
God hears all of my prayers,
Even when I think He has not.

I say I won't give up,
And I won't ever give in.
But God allows everyone
to start over again...

For that's where love begins.

HEAL ME

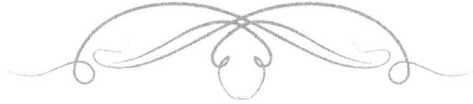

I pray for God to heal my soul,
Divine love makes me whole.

Without God I could fall apart,
A piece of heaven is within my heart.

I have no chains that hold or bind me,
Hope keeps fear far behind me.

No matter how hard my days may get,
I live in faith without regret.

I choose to walk a path of kindness,
For only love is truly timeless.

BELIEVE IN LOVE

When things fall out of place,
Rely on grace.

When you are in despair,
Just say one prayer.

When you have fallen down
Hope can turn you around.

When your grief won't cease,
Hold your faith for peace.

When you have been deprived of,
There is always love.

LOST

I was lost;
I was alone;
Only two feet;
To take me home.

I lost many friends;
I had no place;
Only my thoughts;
An angel's face.

I took one step;
Then another;
My only guide;
The Holy Father.

I had fear;
And I had doubt;
I could only cry;
I couldn't shout.

I gathered strength;
Fell to my knees;
I prayed for hope;
Love set me free.

I followed the light;
To a new day;
For this is how;
I found my way.

AN ANGEL'S THOUGHTS...

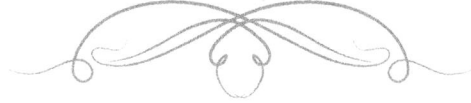

There's no need for you to worry;
You're always in God's hands.

There's no need for you to ask again;
All of your prayers were heard.

There's no need for you to cry;
Your sorrow is felt in my heart.

There's no need for you to give up;
I know where you are going.

You just need to know that I love you
with all the light of my soul.

LIFE

Life is a beautiful opportunity. Enjoy it with love.

Love is a golden gift. Share it with hope.

Hope is a yearning given by God. Carry it with faith.

Faith is a divine blessing.
Believe and you will be blessed with a peaceful life,
filled with both hope and love.

LOVE

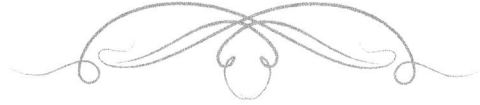

Love is more than all of the kind words
whispered in your ear.

Love is more than a gentle caress of your face.

Love is more than all the beauty
your eyes can behold.

Love is simply the grace that resides in your heart to make you
who you are...

a beautiful soul.

I LOVE...

I love when clouds kiss the blue sky
on a perfect summer day.

I love the oceans and the taste of salt spray.

I love the smiles I give to others
to send them on a happier way.

I love that I'm blessed with people
who've cared about me today.

I love that I'm guided by light
so my soul won't go astray

I love you with every fiber of my being
in the most heartfelt way.

I love... therefore I am.

PARENTS

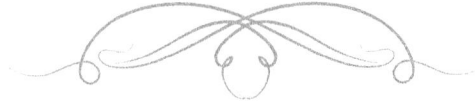

Bills and work might be parental distractions;
But it never diminishes their love and compassion.

Parents are thankful for
the children they've raised;
Even when their kids don't seem to behave.

Without their children, they'd feel all alone;
Sons and daughters make their house a home.

Parents teach their children
lessons of love and care;
When their child is in trouble,
they're always there.

A parent's comfort lives in their
child's laughter and smile;
Every minute they have with their child make it all worthwhile.

A child's happiness is a parent's joy;
Parents are always proud of their girls and boys.

But to lose their child, their hearts need mending;
Until they find a child's love is forever
and never ending.

FAMILY

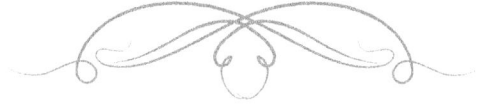

I love you more than you may ever know,
You're a kindred spirit who allowed me to grow.

Growing up together made our house a home,
Without you I would be alone.

You gave me confidence to say I can,
Without you I wouldn't be who I am.

BELIEVE

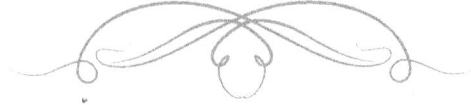

Believe in your community.
You are part of something greater than yourself.

Believe in others.
There are good people out there who care.

Believe in yourself.
You are an amazing soul.

Believe in love.
It's our greatest gift.

Just Believe!

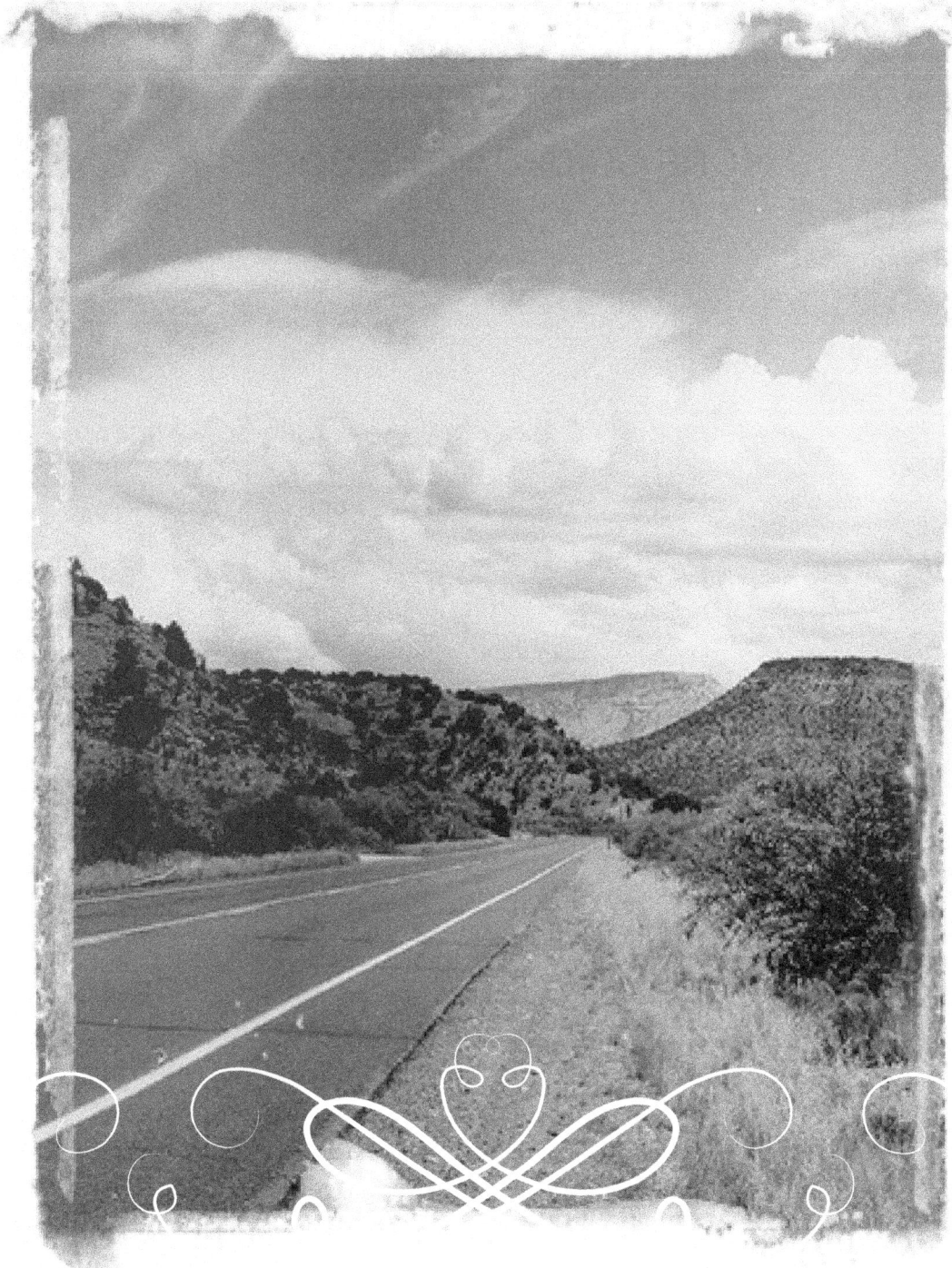

MORE GUIDE TO THE SOUL!

Do you have a compelling story about a kindred spirit, a lesson in compassion, or a captivating view on volunteerism that has changed your life? If so, I invite you to submit your story to be considered for publication in the upcoming follow up books in Guide to the Soul series.

Stories may be up to fifteen hundred words and must be either a lesson in compassion or a captivating story on volunteerism that is uplifting and inspiring. You may submit your own original piece, something you've read, or your favorite inspirational quote.

To obtain a copy of the submission guidelines and submit your story, please visit the Guide to the Soul website at www. guidetothesoul.com or contact us at the address below.

We ensure that all original submissions are credited.

For submissions, guidelines, and more information:

Guide to the Soul Submissions
135 Mohawk Street
Cohoes, NY 12047
Phone: (518) 326-1135

email: submissions@guidetothesoul.com
www.guidetothesoul.com

SPEAKING OPPORTUNITIES

Have the author speak at your next event! Robert Clancy's compelling speaking engagements and learning seminars are now available for your company, charity, or volunteer organization! In his signature keynote speech, Drawing Leadership from the Heart— Lessons in Compassion, Robert uses examples from his books, such as The Hitchhiker's Guide to the Soul, to illustrate how volunteerism, kindness and a compassion for humanity can help shape the future.

For all inquiries please contact us at:

Guide to the Soul, LLC
135 Mohawk Street
Cohoes, NY 12047
Phone: (518) 326-1135

email: inquiries@guidetothesoul.com
www.guidetothesoul.com

ABOUT THE AUTHOR

Robert Clancy is a creative visionary, #1 international bestselling author, spiritual teacher and co-founder of Spiral Design Studio. At age nineteen, Robert had a divine spiritual experience that altered his life in profound ways. In 2012, he created the Guide To The Soul Facebook fan page, where he shares his divinely inspired thoughts, now followed by nearly a million people worldwide.

He is a sought after speaker, presenter and guest. Robert is also a regular contributor and weekly guest on Los Angeles KABC Radio's syndicated *Late Night Health Radio Show*. He's also co-host and producer of *The Mindset Reset TV Show*, which airs in over 160 countries.

His latest book *Soul Cyphers: Decoding a Life of Hope and Happiness* released October 2017 quickly became a #1 international bestseller. Robert is also a featured spiritual expert appearing with Dr. Joe Vitale, don Miguel Ruiz, Brian Tracy and Dannion Brinkley in the movie *Becoming the Keys*, set to release in the February of 2019.

Robert also recently completed his filming of an episode for the 2018-19 season of the Emmy® Award winning *Dr. Nandi Show* which reaches over 300 million people on major cable and satellite television networks such as Discovery and ABC. Robert is a husband, father and 5th Degree Master Black Belt Martial Arts Instructor.

Guide to the Soul, LLC
www.guidetothesoul.com

www.ingramcontent.com/pod-product-compliance
Lightning Source LLC
Chambersburg PA
CBHW062105090426

42741CB00015B/3334